Your Promise of Success

Welcome to the world of Confident Cooking, created for you in our test kitchen, where recipes are double-tested by our team of home economists to achieve a high standard of success.

MURDOCH BOOKS®
Sydney • London • Vancouver • New York

~ Classic Sponge ~

Preparation time:
20 minutes
Total cooking time:
20 minutes

Makes one 20 cm round layer cake

1/2 cup plain flour
1/2 cup self-raising flour
4 eggs, separated
2/3 cup caster sugar
1/2 cup strawberry jam
1/2 cup cream, whipped

1~Preheat oven to moderate 180°C. Brush 2 shallow 20 cm sandwich tins with melted butter or oil. Line bases of tins with baking paper. Sift flours together three times onto a sheet of greaseproof paper. Place egg whites in a large clean, dry bowl. Using electric beaters, beat until firm peaks form. Add sugar gradually, beating constantly until sugar is dissolved and mixture is thick and glossy.

2~Add the egg yolks, beat for another 20 seconds. Fold in flour quickly and lightly with a metal spoon.

3~Spread mixture evenly in prepared tins. Bake for 20 minutes, until lightly golden and springy to touch. Leave the sponges in tins for 5 minutes before turning onto wire racks to cool.

4~Spread jam evenly onto one of the sponges. Using a fluted nozzle, pipe whipped cream in rosettes over jam. Top with second sponge, and dust with sifted icing sugar before serving.

Storage time~Unfilled sponges can be frozen for up to one month; freeze in separate freezer bags. Thaw sponges at room temperature (for about 20 minutes). A filled sponge is best served immediately.

Hint~The secret to making a perfect sponge lies in the folding technique. Use only a large metal spoon, working quickly yet gently to incorporate the flour. A beating action, or using a wooden spoon, will cause loss of volume in the egg mixture and will result in a flat, heavy cake.

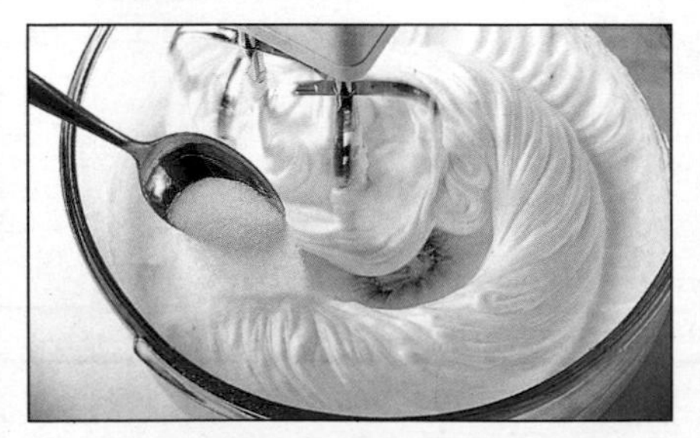

Add the sugar gradually to the beaten egg white, beating constantly.

Fold in the flour quickly and lightly with a metal spoon.

Bake sponge until it is lightly golden on top and springy to touch.

Pipe whipped cream rosettes over jam on top of the cake.

~ Cinnamon Teacake ~

Preparation time:
20 minutes
Total cooking time:
30 minutes

Makes one 20 cm cake

60 g butter
1/2 cup caster sugar
1 egg, lightly beaten
1 teaspoon vanilla essence
3/4 cup self-raising flour
1/4 cup plain flour
1/2 cup milk

Topping
20 g butter, melted
1 tablespoon caster sugar
1 teaspoon ground cinnamon

1~Preheat oven to moderate 180°C. Brush a 20 cm round shallow cake tin with melted butter or oil; line base with baking paper. Using electric beaters, beat the butter and sugar in a small bowl until light and creamy. Add egg gradually, beating well after each addition. Add the essence and beat until combined.

2~Transfer mixture to a large mixing bowl. Using a metal spoon, fold in sifted flours alternately with milk. Stir until smooth. Spoon into prepared tin and smooth surface. Bake for 30 minutes or until a skewer comes out clean when inserted into centre of cake. Stand cake in tin 5 minutes before turning out onto a wire rack to cool.

3~While cake is still warm, brush top with melted butter and sprinkle with combined sugar and cinnamon.

~ Carrot Cake ~

Preparation time:
30 minutes
Total cooking time:
1 hour

Makes one 20 cm square cake

2 cups grated carrot
1/2 cup sultanas
2/3 cup chopped walnuts
1 cup caster sugar
3 eggs, lightly beaten
3/4 cup vegetable oil
2 cups self-raising flour
2 teaspoons mixed spice
2 teaspoons ground ginger
1 teaspoon ground cinnamon
1 teaspoon bicarbonate of soda

Icing
185 g cream cheese
1/3 cup icing sugar

1~Preheat oven to moderate 180°C. Brush deep 20 cm square cake tin with melted butter or oil; line base with baking paper. Place carrot, sultanas, walnuts and sugar in large bowl. Add combined eggs and oil.

2~Add sifted flour, spices and soda. Combine with wooden spoon.

3~Pour into prepared tin, smooth surface. Bake for 1 hour or until skewer comes out clean when inserted into

Cinnamon Teacake (top) and Carrot Cake

centre. Leave in tin for 10 minutes before turning onto wire rack.

4∼To make Icing: Using electric beaters, beat the cream cheese and sugar in a small bowl until light and creamy. Spread on top of cooled cake. Dust with mixed spice or nutmeg, if desired.

Variation∼Add a teaspoon of grated lemon rind to icing.

~ Favourite Chocolate Cake ~

Preparation time:
20 minutes
Total cooking time:
1 hour

Makes 1 loaf cake

185 g butter
3/4 cup caster sugar
2 eggs, lightly beaten
1 cup self-raising flour
3/4 cup plain flour
1/2 cup cocoa powder
1 teaspoon bicarbonate of soda
1/2 cup milk

Icing
30 g butter, melted
2 tablespoons hot water
2 tablespoons cocoa powder
1 cup icing sugar

1~Preheat oven to moderate 180°C. Brush a 21 x 14 x 7 cm loaf tin with melted butter or oil. Line base and sides with baking paper. Using electric beaters, beat butter and sugar in a small bowl until light and creamy. Add eggs gradually, beating well after each addition.

2~Transfer mixture to a large mixing bowl. Using a metal spoon, fold in sifted flours, cocoa powder and bicarbonate of soda alternately with milk; stir until smooth. Spoon mixture into prepared loaf tin; smooth surface.

3~Bake for 1 hour, until a skewer comes out clean when inserted into centre of cake. Leave in tin for 5 minutes before turning onto a wire rack to cool.

4~To make Icing: Combine butter, water and cocoa in a medium mixing bowl; mix to a smooth paste; add sifted icing sugar. Stir until all the ingredients are combined and mixture is smooth. Spread icing onto cooled cake and dust with icing sugar.

Storage time~ Favourite Chocolate Cake can be stored in the freezer for up to one month, un-iced and sealed in plastic wrap.

Variation~For a richer tasting cake, substitute 50 g dark chocolate for the hot water and cocoa powder when making the icing. Combine the chocolate and butter in a small heatproof bowl. Stand bowl over a pan of hot water and stir until chocolate has melted. Add chocolate mixture to the sifted icing sugar and stir until the mixture is smooth. Spread icing onto the cooled cake and decorate with chocolate curls, if desired.

Line base and sides of greased loaf tin with baking paper.

Fold in the sifted dry ingredients with a metal spoon.

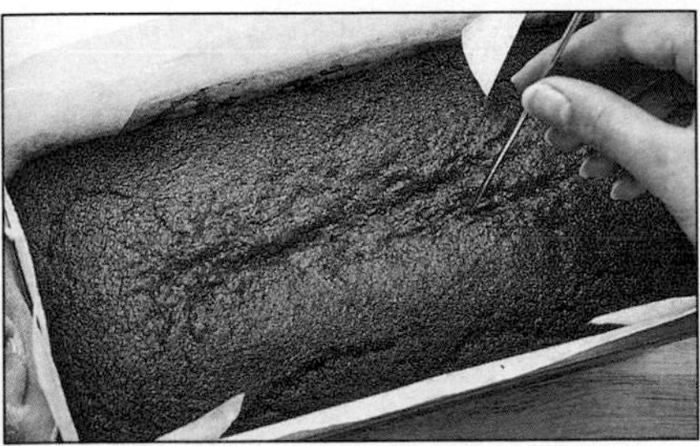

Test with a skewer to see if cake is baked—it should come out clean.

Stir icing mixture until it is smooth and ingredients are well combined.

~ Cherry Cake ~

Preparation time:
30 minutes
Total cooking time:
45 minutes

Makes one 20 cm fluted ring cake

1 cup glacé cherries
90 g butter
2/3 cup sugar
2 eggs, lightly beaten
1 teaspoon vanilla essence
1 cup self-raising flour
2/3 cup plain flour
1/3 cup milk

Icing
1 cup icing sugar
20 g butter
1–2 tablespoons water
pink food colouring

1~Preheat oven to moderate 180°C. Brush a 20 cm fluted ring tin with oil or melted butter. Dust lightly with flour, shake off excess. Place glacé cherries in a strainer and wash under running water to remove syrup. Pat dry with paper towel. Using electric beaters, beat butter and sugar in a small mixing bowl until light and creamy. Add eggs gradually, beating well after each addition. Add essence; beat until combined.

2~Transfer mixture to a large mixing bowl. Using metal spoon, fold in the sifted flours alternately with milk. Stir until combined and mixture is smooth.

3~Spoon mixture into prepared tin; smooth surface. Bake 35 minutes, until skewer comes out clean when inserted into centre of cake. Leave in tin for 10 minutes before turning onto a wire rack to cool.

4~**To make Icing:** Combine sifted icing sugar, butter and water in small heatproof bowl. Stand bowl over a pan of simmering water, stirring mixture until butter has melted and the icing is glossy and smooth. Add a couple of drops of pink food colouring and stir to combine. Using a spoon, drizzle icing over top of cake, allowing it to run freely down the sides.

Storage time~This cake will keep for up to 2 days in an airtight container in the refrigerator. It can be frozen, without icing, for up to one month.

Variation~Sprinkle icing, before it sets, with desiccated coconut.

Pat the washed glacé cherries dry with paper towel.

Fold in the sifted flours alternately with milk, using a metal spoon.

Test to see if the cake is cooked by inserting a metal skewer into the centre.

Add a couple of drops of pink food colouring to the icing mixture and stir.

~ Dobos Torte ~

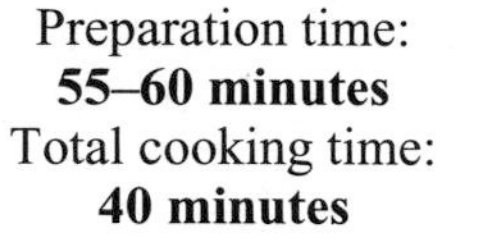

Preparation time:
55–60 minutes
Total cooking time:
40 minutes

Serves 12

8 eggs, separated	**100 g dark chocolate, melted**
1 cup caster sugar	**250 g unsalted butter**
1 1/2 cups plain flour	
Filling	***Toffee***
1 1/2 cups caster sugar	**1 cup caster sugar**
1/2 cup water	**1/2 cup water**
5 egg yolks	**125 g flaked almonds, toasted**
1/4 cup cocoa powder	

1 ~ Preheat oven to moderate 180°C. Line six baking trays with baking paper and draw a 23 cm circle on each sheet of paper. Using electric beaters, beat egg yolks and half the sugar for 20 minutes or until thick and pale. Beat egg whites until stiff peaks form. Gradually add remaining sugar, beating until mixture is thick and glossy and sugar has dissolved. Sift flour onto beaten egg yolk. Fold in gently with metal spoon. Fold in egg whites a third at a time. Spread mixture evenly onto the circles on trays. Bake for 6–9 minutes or until cakes are lightly golden and top of each cake springs back when lightly touched. Turn onto wire racks; cool, then trim edges evenly.

2 ~ To make Filling: Place sugar and water in medium pan. Stir until sugar dissolves. Bring to boil, reduce heat and simmer 10–15 minutes or until syrup reaches soft-ball stage. Using electric beaters, beat egg yolks in a medium bowl. Gradually pour hot syrup onto egg yolks in a thin stream, beating constantly; continue beating until mixture is cool and thick. Add cocoa, beating until smooth. Add melted chocolate, beating until well combined. Beat butter until light and creamy; gradually add egg mixture, beat until blended and smooth.

3 ~ To make Toffee: Place sugar and water in a heavy-based pan, stir over low heat until sugar has dissolved. Boil without stirring for 5–10 minutes or until syrup turns golden. Pour onto one of the cakes.

Divide the cake mixture evenly and spread in a circle on each sheet of baking paper.

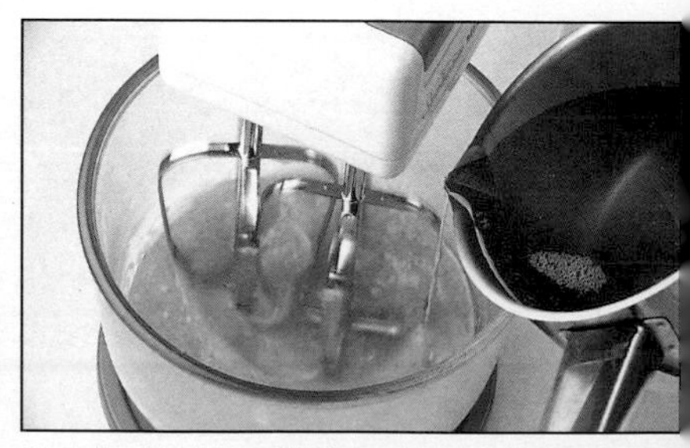

Gradually pour the hot sugar syrup onto the beaten egg yolks in a thin stream.

Spread caramel quickly and evenly; cut into 12 equal wedges while still soft with hot, oiled, sharp knife.

4~To assemble the cake, spread filling over remaining cakes, reserving enough to cover sides. Sandwich cakes together, placing caramel layer on top. Spread sides evenly with filling, press toasted almonds around sides.

Boil sugar and water without stirring until it forms a golden-coloured syrup.

Spread chocolate filling over remaining cakes, keeping enough for the sides.

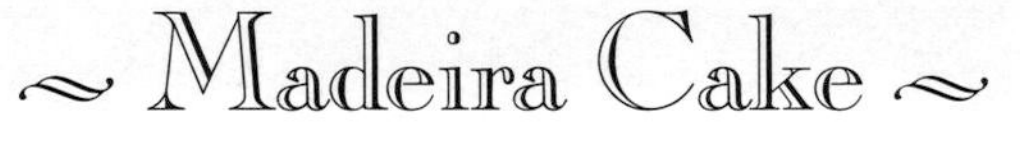

~ Madeira Cake ~

Preparation time:
20 minutes
Total cooking time:
55 minutes

Makes one loaf cake

150 g butter
3/4 cup caster sugar
3 eggs, lightly beaten
2 teaspoons finely grated orange or lemon rind
1/2 cup ground almonds
1 3/4 cups self-raising flour
icing sugar, for dusting

1~Preheat oven to moderate 180°C. Brush a 23 x 13 x 7 cm loaf tin with melted butter or oil. Line base and sides with baking paper. Using electric beaters, beat butter and sugar in a small mixing bowl until light and creamy. Add the eggs gradually, beating thoroughly after each addition. Add rind, beat until combined.
2~Transfer mixture to a large bowl. Using a metal spoon, fold in ground almonds and sifted flour. Stir until combined and smooth.
3~Spoon into prepared tin; smooth surface. Bake for 55 minutes or until skewer comes out clean when inserted into centre of cake.
4~Leave cake in tin for 10 minutes before turning out onto wire rack. Dust top with icing sugar before serving.
Storage time~Cake will keep up to four days in an airtight container.

~ Date and Nut Rolls ~

Preparation time:
25 minutes
Total cooking time:
1 hour

Makes two rolls

3/4 cup self-raising flour
3/4 cup plain flour
1/2 teaspoon bicarbonate of soda
1 teaspoon mixed spice
1 cup chopped walnuts
100 g butter
3/4 cup soft brown sugar
1/2 cup water
1 1/2 cups chopped dates
1 egg, lightly beaten

1~Preheat oven to moderate 180°C. Brush two 17 x 8 cm tube tins (nut roll tins) and lids with melted butter or oil. Sift flours, soda and spice into a large mixing bowl. Add walnuts, stir to combine and make a well in the centre.
2~Combine butter, sugar, water and dates in a medium pan. Stir over a low heat until butter has melted and sugar has dissolved. Remove from heat and cool slightly.
3~Add butter mixture and egg to mixing bowl, stir until combined. Spoon mixture evenly into prepared tins. Bake with the tins upright for 1 hour or until skewer comes out clean when inserted into centre. Leave cakes in tins, with lids on, for 10 minutes, then turn onto wire rack. Serve sliced with butter.

Madeira Cake (top) and Date and Nut Roll

~ Honey Cream Roll ~

Preparation time:
40 minutes
Total cooking time:
12 minutes

Makes one roll

$^3/_4$ cup self-raising flour
2 teaspoons mixed spice
3 eggs
$^2/_3$ cup soft brown sugar
$^1/_4$ cup desiccated coconut

Honey Cream
125 g unsalted butter
$^1/_3$ cup caster sugar
2 tablespoons honey

1~Preheat oven to moderately hot 210°C. Brush a 30 x 25 x 2 cm swiss roll tin with melted butter or oil; line the base with baking paper, extending up two sides. Sift flour and spice three times onto a sheet of greaseproof paper. Using electric beaters, beat the eggs in a large mixing bowl for 5 minutes until thick, frothy and pale. Add sugar gradually, beating constantly until sugar is dissolved and mixture is pale and glossy. Fold in flour quickly and lightly, using a metal spoon.

2~Spread mixture evenly in the prepared tin; smooth the surface. Bake for 12 minutes, until the cake is lightly golden and springy to touch. Lay out a clean, dry tea-towel, cover with greaseproof paper and sprinkle paper with coconut. Turn cooked cake onto coconut and leave for 1 minute.

3~Using the tea-towel as a guide, carefully roll cake, along with paper, up from the short side; leave for 5 minutes or until cool. Unroll cake, discard paper. Spread with Honey Cream, re-roll; trim ends with a knife. Serve sliced.

4~**To make Honey Cream:** Using electric beaters, beat butter, sugar and honey in a small mixing bowl until light and creamy. Remove bowl from electric mixer. Cover mixture with cold water, swirl water around and pour off. Beat mixture again with electric beaters for another 2 minutes. Repeat this process six times until the cream is white and fluffy and the sugar has completely dissolved.

Add the sugar gradually to the beaten eggs, beating until pale and glossy.

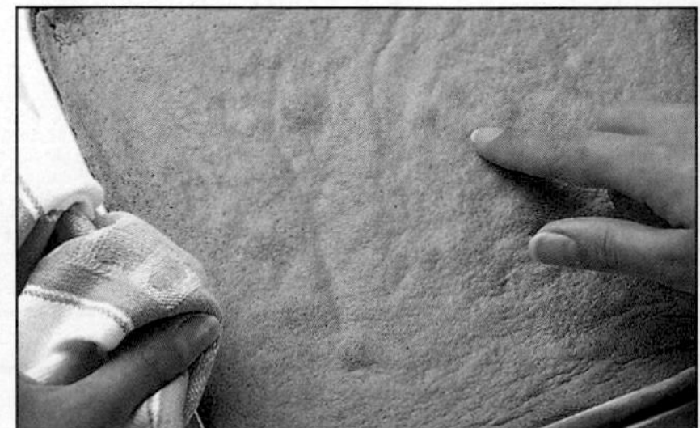

Bake the cake until lightly golden on top and springy to touch.

Roll the cake up with greaseproof paper, using the tea-towel as a guide.

Cover the creamed butter mixture with cold water, swirl around and pour off.

~ Angel Food Cake ~

Preparation time:
25 minutes
Total cooking time:
45 minutes

Makes one 23 cm ring cake

2/3 cup plain flour
1/4 cup cornflour
2/3 cup caster sugar
10 egg whites
1 1/2 teaspoons cream of tartar
1 cup caster sugar, extra
1 teaspoon vanilla essence

Frosting
1 1/4 cups caster sugar
1/2 cup water
3 egg whites

1~Preheat oven to moderate 180°C. Sift flour and cornflour twice onto a sheet of greaseproof paper. Add caster sugar and sift again. Using electric beaters, beat egg whites in a large bowl until soft peaks form. Add cream of tartar and beat until combined.

2~Add sugar gradually, beating constantly until it has dissolved and the mixture is thick and glossy. Add essence and beat until combined.

3~Using a metal spoon, fold in flour in three batches, until just combined. Spoon mixture into a 23 cm angel food cake tin. Bake for 45 minutes, until lightly golden and springy to the touch. Invert cake tin onto a board and leave tin on until cake cools completely. Run a knife around side of cake to loosen; turn onto a large plate. Cover top and sides with Frosting and decorate with gilded sugared almonds (dragées), if desired.

4~**To make Frosting:** Combine sugar and water in a small pan. Stir constantly over low heat until mixture boils and sugar has dissolved. Simmer, uncovered, without stirring, for 5 minutes. Using electric beaters, beat egg whites in a clean, dry mixing bowl until stiff peaks form. Pour hot syrup over egg whites, beating constantly until icing is thick, glossy and increased in volume.

Storage time~Cake will keep up to two days in an airtight container.

Note~This cake is traditionally baked in a special Angel Food Cake tin or 'tube pan', available at specialty kitchen supply shops or large department stores.

Sift the flour and cornflour twice onto a sheet of greaseproof paper.

Add vanilla essence to the beaten egg white and sugar mixture.

Invert the cake tin onto a board and leave it until the cake cools completely.

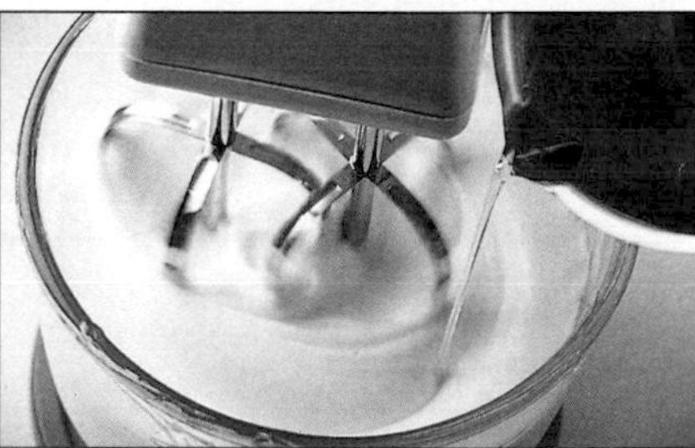

Pour hot sugar syrup in a thin stream into egg whites, beating constantly.

~ Mocha Genoise Gateau ~

Preparation time:
40 minutes
Total cooking time:
40 minutes

Makes one 23 cm round layer cake

1 cup plain flour	**2 tablespoons instant coffee powder**
4 eggs	**1 tablespoon hot water**
2/3 cup caster sugar	
60 g butter, melted and cooled	**2 tablespoons crème de cacao**
Mocha Buttercream	**1 cup flaked almonds, toasted**
1/2 cup caster sugar	**coffee beans, chocolate-coated or plain roasted, to decorate**
1/3 cup water	
4 egg yolks	
250 g butter, softened	

1~Preheat oven to moderate 180°C. Brush a deep 23 cm round cake tin with oil or melted butter; line base and sides with baking paper. Sift flour three times onto a sheet of greaseproof paper. Using electric beaters, beat eggs and sugar in a large mixing bowl for 6 minutes or until the mixture is thick and pale and has increased in volume. Using a metal spoon, quickly and lightly fold in flour in two batches until ingredients are just combined. Add melted butter, discarding any white sediment, with the second batch. Spread mixture evenly in the prepared tin and bake for 35 minutes, until lightly golden and springy to the touch. Leave cake in tin for 2 minutes before turning onto a wire rack to cool. Remove the paper.

2~**To make Mocha Buttercream:** Combine sugar and water in a small pan. Stir mixture constantly over medium heat without boiling until the sugar has completely dissolved. Bring to the boil, reduce heat slightly and simmer without stirring for 5 minutes. Remove syrup from heat and cool slightly. Using electric beaters, beat egg yolks for 2 minutes. Slowly pour the syrup onto the yolks, beating constantly until the mixture is cool. Gradually add butter to the cooled mixture, beating constantly until smooth and creamy. Add the coffee dissolved in hot water and beat until combined. To assemble the cake, cut it in half horizontally, using a serrated knife. Brush crème de cacao on top of each cake half. Spread a quarter of the buttercream on the bottom layer and replace top layer. Spread two-thirds of remaining buttercream over top and sides of cake, smoothing surfaces. Press flaked almonds onto sides of cake. Place remaining buttercream in a piping bag fitted with a fluted nozzle. Pipe swirls of buttercream around the top edge of the cake. Decorate swirls with small coffee beans and pieces of choc-mint sticks, if desired.

Storage time~This cake will keep for up to three days sealed in an airtight container.

Note~A genoise is a classic whisked cake, very light and moist.

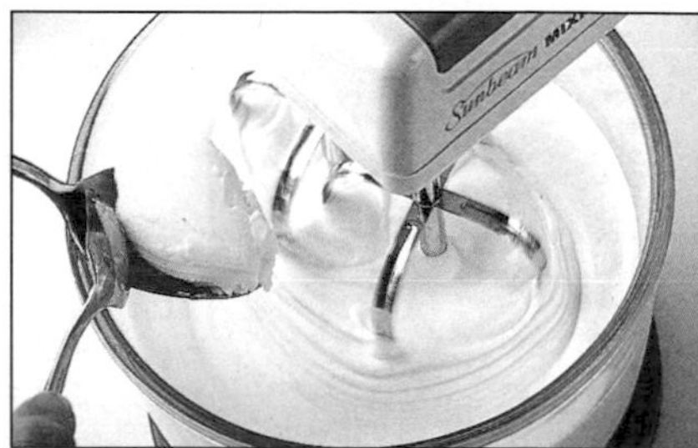

When cake has cooled on wire rack, carefully remove baking paper.

Gradually add butter to the cooled beaten egg yolk and syrup mixture.

~ Semolina Lemon Syrup Cake ~

Preparation time:
30 minutes
Total cooking time:
50 minutes

Makes one 23 cm ring cake

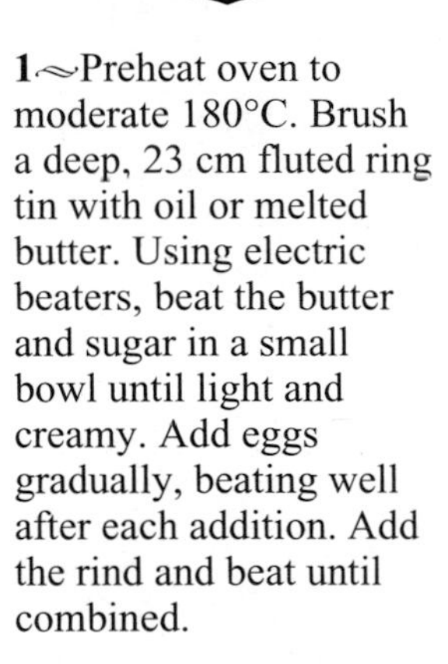

150 g butter
3/4 cup caster sugar
2 eggs, lightly beaten
2 teaspoons finely grated lemon rind
1 1/2 cups finely ground semolina
1 cup ground almonds
1 1/2 teaspoons baking powder
1/4 cup milk

Lemon Syrup
1/2 cup lemon juice
rind of 1 lemon
1/2 cup caster sugar

1~Preheat oven to moderate 180°C. Brush a deep, 23 cm fluted ring tin with oil or melted butter. Using electric beaters, beat the butter and sugar in a small bowl until light and creamy. Add eggs gradually, beating well after each addition. Add the rind and beat until combined.

2~Transfer mixture to a large bowl. Using a metal spoon, fold in combined semolina, almonds and baking powder alternately with milk. Stir until smooth.

3~Spoon into prepared tin, smooth surface. Bake for 45 minutes or until a skewer comes out clean when inserted in centre. Leave cake in tin 5 minutes, turn onto a serving plate. Brush syrup over top and sides of cake; cool and dust with sifted icing sugar.

4~**To make Lemon Syrup:** Combine juice, rind and sugar in a small pan. Stir over a medium heat without boiling until sugar dissolves. Bring to boil, reduce heat, simmer 5 minutes.

~ Spiced Struesel Cake ~

Preparation time:
30 minutes
Total cooking time:
50 minutes

Makes one 20 cm cake

2 cups self-raising flour
1 teaspoon ground cinnamon
1 teaspoon ground ginger
1/2 teaspoon ground cardamom
1/2 teaspoon ground cloves
185 g butter
3/4 cup soft brown sugar
1/4 cup golden syrup
3 eggs, lightly beaten
1/4 cup buttermilk
2 tablespoons soft brown sugar, extra
1 teaspoon mixed spice
1/3 cup finely chopped walnuts

1~Preheat oven to moderate 180°C. Brush a deep 20 cm springform pan with oil or melted butter, line base and sides with baking paper. Sift flour and spices into a large mixing bowl. Make a well in centre. Combine butter, sugar and golden syrup in a medium pan. Stir over

Semolina Lemon Syrup Cake (top) and Spiced Struesel Cake

low heat until butter has melted and mixture is smooth. Remove from heat and cool slightly.

2~Add butter mixture to bowl; using a wooden spoon, stir until just combined. Add combined eggs and buttermilk, stir until just combined and mixture is smooth.

3~Pour mixture into prepared tin, smooth surface. Combine extra sugar, spice and walnuts, spread over surface of mixture; press in lightly.

4~Bake for 45 minutes or until a skewer comes out clean when inserted into centre of cake. Leave in tin 15 minutes before removing.

Storage time~Store for up to three days in an airtight container.

~ Devil's Food Cake ~

Preparation time:
25 minutes
Total cooking time:
1 hour

Makes one 20 cm round layer cake

1 cup plain flour
1 cup self-raising flour
1 teaspoon bicarbonate of soda
2/3 cup cocoa powder
1 1/4 cups caster sugar
125 g butter, softened
1 cup milk
1 cup sour cream
3 eggs, lightly beaten
3/4 cup cream, whipped

Chocolate Icing
50 g dark chocolate
25 g butter
3 teaspoons icing sugar

1~Preheat oven to moderate 180°C. Brush a deep 20 cm round cake tin with oil or melted butter. Sift flours, soda and cocoa powder into a large mixing bowl. Add sugar, butter, milk and sour cream; beat for 1 minute at medium speed until combined.

2~Add eggs, increase speed to high and beat for 4 minutes until smooth and creamy. Pour into prepared tin and bake for 1 hour or until a skewer comes out clean when inserted into centre. Remove cake from oven and leave in tin for 10 minutes before turning onto a wire rack.

3~To make Icing: Combine chocolate and butter in a small heatproof bowl. Stand bowl over a pan of simmering water and stir until mixture is melted and smooth. Gradually add the sifted icing sugar, stirring until icing is smooth.

4~When the cake is cold, cut it in half horizontally, using a serrated knife, and spread whipped cream on the bottom layer. Replace the top layer. Spread top of the cake evenly with a layer of chocolate icing.

Note~ When melting chocolate, do not let any water or steam come into contact with the mixture or it will 'seize' into a rough mass and become unworkable. If this happens, you will need to discard the chocolate and start the process again.

Add the sugar, butter, milk and sour cream to the flour and cocoa powder.

After adding eggs, beat the mixture for four minutes until smooth and creamy.

Gradually add the sifted icing sugar to the butter and chocolate mixture.

Cut cold cake horizontally in half and spread cream on bottom layer.

~ Almond Cake ~

Preparation time:
20 minutes
Total cooking time:
45 minutes

Makes one 17 cm round cake

125 g butter
2/3 cup caster sugar
2 drops almond essence
3 eggs, lightly beaten
90 g ground almonds
1/2 cup plain flour
whole almonds for decoration

1~Preheat oven to moderate 180°C. Brush a deep 17 cm round sandwich tin with melted butter or oil. Line base with baking paper. Using electric beaters, beat butter, sugar and essence in small mixing bowl until light and creamy.

2~Add one third of eggs, together with one third of ground almonds; repeat with remaining eggs and almonds.

3~Using metal spoon, fold in sifted flour; stir until ingredients are combined and the mixture is smooth.

4~Spoon mixture into prepared tin; smooth surface, decorate with almonds. Bake for 45 minutes or until skewer comes out clean when inserted into centre of cake. Leave cake in tin for 10 minutes; turn onto a wire rack to cool. Dust with caster sugar or icing sugar to serve.

Storage time~Cake will keep for three days in airtight container or two months in freezer.

~ Seed Cake ~

Preparation time:
20 minutes
Total cooking time:
50 minutes

Makes one 17 cm round cake

125 g butter
1/2 cup caster sugar
3 eggs, lightly beaten
1 1/4 cups self-raising flour
3 teaspoons caraway seeds
2 tablespoons milk

1~Preheat oven to moderate 180°C. Brush base and sides of a deep 17 cm round cake tin with oil or melted butter. Line base with baking paper. Using electric beaters, beat butter and sugar in small mixing bowl until light and creamy. Add eggs gradually, beating thoroughly after each addition.

2~Transfer mixture to a large bowl; use a metal spoon to fold in sifted flour and caraway seeds alternately with milk.

3~Spoon into prepared tin, smooth surface. Bake for 50 minutes or until a skewer comes out clean when inserted in centre; leave cake in tin for 20 minutes before turning onto wire rack to cool. Serve plain or dust with icing sugar.

Storage time~One week in an airtight container, or up to three months in the freezer.

Note~Seed Cake is a traditional English cake made to celebrate the end of Spring sowing of the crop.

Almond Cake (top) and Seed Cake

~ Ginger Cake ~

Preparation time:
30 minutes
Total cooking time:
$3/4$–1 hour

Makes one 20 cm square cake

125 g butter
$1/2$ cup black treacle
$1/2$ cup golden syrup
$1\,1/2$ cups plain flour
1 cup self-raising flour
1 teaspoon bicarbonate of soda
3 teaspoons ground ginger
1 teaspoon mixed spice
$1/4$ teaspoon ground cinnamon
$3/4$ cup soft brown sugar
1 cup milk
2 eggs, lightly beaten

Lemon Ginger Icing
$1\,3/4$ cups icing sugar
1 teaspoon ground ginger
30 g butter, melted
2 teaspoons milk
2 teaspoons lemon juice
1 teaspoon lemon rind

1~Preheat oven to moderate 180°C. Brush a deep 20 cm square cake tin with oil or melted butter. Line base with baking paper. Combine butter, treacle and syrup in a medium pan; stir over low heat until butter has melted; remove from heat.
2~Sift flours, soda and spices into a large mixing bowl; add the sugar; stir until well combined. Make a well in the centre; add butter mixture to dry ingredients, together with combined milk and eggs. Using a wooden spoon, stir until mixture is smooth and ingredients are well combined.
3~Pour into prepared tin; smooth surface. Bake 45 minutes–1 hour or until skewer comes out clean when inserted into centre. Leave in tin 20 minutes, turn out onto wire rack to cool.
4~To make Lemon Ginger Icing: Combine sifted icing sugar, ginger, butter, milk, lemon juice and rind in a small bowl; mix to form a paste. Stand bowl over pan of simmering water, stir until icing is smooth and glossy; remove from heat. Spread over top of cake with a flat-bladed knife. Decorate with shredded lemon rind or glacé ginger, if desired.
Storage time~ Cake is best served 2–3 days after making. Store for up to a week in an airtight container, or freeze for up to three months, un-iced.

Combine the butter, treacle and golden syrup in a medium pan.

Pour combined milk and eggs, along with the butter mixture, onto dry ingredients.

After leaving cake in tin for 20 minutes, turn onto a wire rack to cool.

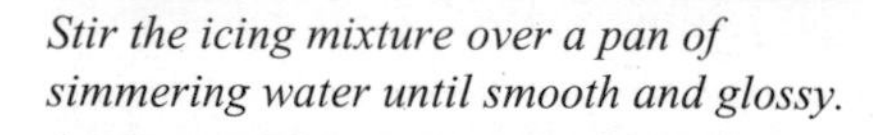

Stir the icing mixture over a pan of simmering water until smooth and glossy.

~ Black Forest Cake ~

Preparation time:
45 minutes
Total cooking time:
15 minutes

Makes one 20 cm layer cake

1/3 cup plain flour
1/3 cup self-raising flour
2 tablespoons cocoa powder
4 eggs, separated
1/2 cup caster sugar
1/4 cup Kirsch
1 1/2 cups cream, whipped
425 g can pitted cherries, well drained
125 g dark chocolate
maraschino cherries on stalks, to decorate

1~Preheat oven to moderate 180°C. Brush two shallow 20 cm round sandwich tins with oil or melted butter. Line base and sides with baking paper. Sift flours and cocoa powder three times onto greaseproof paper. Place egg whites in a small, clean, dry mixing bowl. Using electric beaters, beat until firm peaks form. Add sugar gradually, beating constantly until sugar has dissolved and mixture is thick and glossy. Add yolks, beat for another 20 seconds. Transfer mixture to a larger bowl.

2~Fold in flours and cocoa quickly and lightly. Spread the mixture evenly into prepared tins. Bake for 15 minutes, until cakes are springy to the touch. Leave cakes in tins for 5 minutes before turning them onto wire racks to cool. Cut a dome from the top of each cake and invert so that the base of each cake becomes its upper surface.

3~Brush the top of each cake liberally with Kirsch. Spread a quarter of the whipped cream onto one cake, cover with cherries. Place the other cake on top. Using a flat-bladed knife, cover cake completely with whipped cream.

4~Using a vegetable peeler, shave curls from the edge of chocolate block. Press chocolate curls lightly onto cream around side of cake. Decorate top of cake with maraschino cherries and extra chocolate curls.

Note~Black Forest Cake is traditionally made with fresh Morello cherries, poached in a sugar syrup and pitted. Canned, pitted cherries are a good substitute.

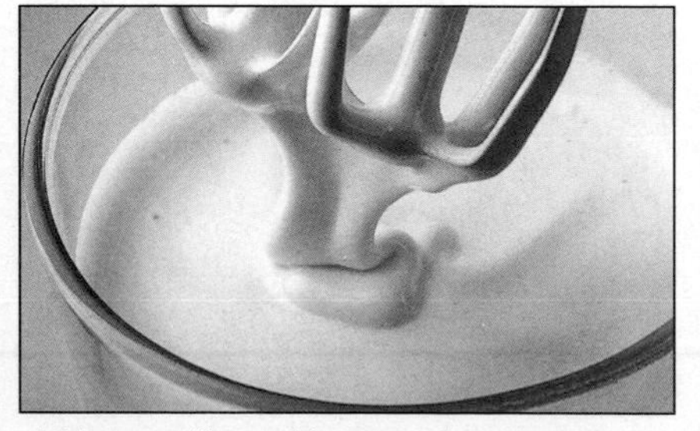

Add egg yolks and beat until mixture is thick and pale and increased in volume.

Spread the cake mixture evenly into the prepared tins.

Place cherries on top of the whipped cream on one cake to form filling.

Shave curls from the edge of a chocolate block to decorate the cake.

~ Yoghurt Citrus Syrup Cake ~

Preparation time:
40 minutes
Total cooking time:
1¼ hours

Makes one 23 cm round cake

180 g butter
1 cup caster sugar
3 teaspoons grated lemon rind
3 teaspoons grated orange rind
5 eggs, separated
1 cup plain yoghurt
2½ cups plain flour
2½ teaspoons baking powder
½ teaspoon bicarbonate of soda

Citrus Syrup
1 cup sugar
¾ cup cold water
1 large piece of lemon rind
1 tablespoon lemon juice
1 tablespoon orange juice
1 tablespoon orange flower water

1~Preheat oven to moderate 180°C. Brush a deep, 23 cm round cake tin with oil or melted butter. Line base with baking paper. Using electric beaters, beat butter, sugar, lemon and orange rinds in a small mixing bowl until light and creamy. Add egg yolks gradually, beating thoroughly after each addition. Transfer mixture to a large bowl. Using a metal spoon, fold in the yoghurt, then combined sifted flour, baking powder and soda. Place egg whites in a small, clean, dry mixing bowl. Using electric beaters, beat until firm peaks form. Using a metal spoon, fold the egg whites quickly into butter mixture. Spoon into prepared tin; smooth surface. Bake for 45–50 minutes or until skewer comes out clean when inserted in centre of cake. Leave the cake in the tin for 5 minutes before pouring syrup over it.

2~**To make Syrup:** Combine sugar and water in a small pan. Stir constantly over low heat until the sugar has dissolved. Bring to boil, then reduce heat and add the rind and juices. Simmer without stirring, uncovered, for 20 minutes. Remove the rind and cool the syrup. Add orange flower water. Pour the Syrup over the cake while it is still in the tin. When all the Syrup has been absorbed, turn the cake out of the tin. Cut into small, thick fingers to serve.

Storage time~Yoghurt Citrus Syrup Cake will keep for three days in an airtight container and for up to two months, without the Citrus Syrup added, in the freezer. Thaw the cake before pouring Syrup over top.

Hint~This cake is delicious served warm, in wedges, with whipped or thick cream.

Variation~Substitute lime rind and lime juice for the lemon rind and juice when making the Citrus Syrup. Use lime rind instead of lemon rind in cake as well.

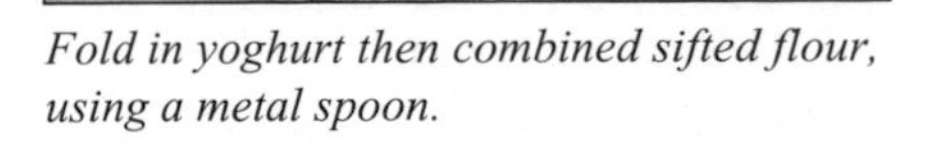

Fold in yoghurt then combined sifted flour, using a metal spoon.

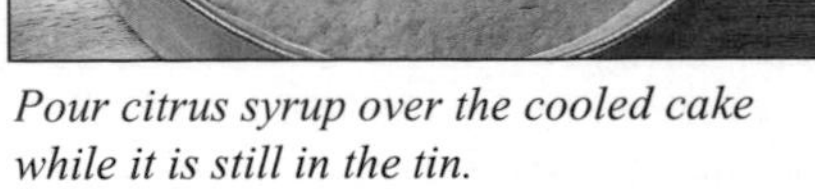

Pour citrus syrup over the cooled cake while it is still in the tin.

~ Siena Cake ~

Preparation time:
30 minutes
Total cooking time:
35-40 minutes

Makes one 23 cm round cake

1 cup roasted blanched almonds
1 cup roasted hazelnuts
1/2 cup glacé apricots, chopped
1/2 cup glacé pineapple, chopped
1/4 cup mixed peel
1/2 cup dried figs, chopped
3/4 cup plain flour
1 tablespoon cocoa powder
1 teaspoon ground cinnamon
1/2 teaspoon mixed spice
1/2 cup caster sugar
1/2 cup honey

1~Preheat oven to slow 150°C. Brush a 23 cm shallow round cake tin with oil or melted butter. Line base and sides with baking paper, extending 1 cm above tin.

2~In a large bowl, combine nuts and chopped fruit. Sift flour, cocoa and spices over the top of the nuts and fruit; coat the nuts and fruit with the flour mixture.

3~Heat sugar and honey in a small pan. Stir over low heat until sugar is dissolved; boil for 1 minute. Pour the hot syrup over the fruit and nut mixture. Using a metal spoon, combine ingredients quickly – the mixture will be very stiff and sticky.

4~Press mixture into prepared tin; spread evenly with wet fingers. Bake for 35–40 minutes. Leave cake in the tin until cold, then turn out and remove the paper. Wrap the cake in foil and leave for at least 2 days before cutting. To serve, sift icing sugar liberally over top of cake and cut it into very small wedges.

Storage time~Siena Cake will keep for up to three months wrapped in foil in the refrigerator.

Note~This flat cake comes from the Italian town of Siena. Also known as panforte, it is especially delicious with coffee and makes a beautiful gift for Christmas, wrapped in festive paper and tied with ribbon. The quantity of ingredients given above will also make two smaller cakes, if preferred. Use two 17 cm tins.

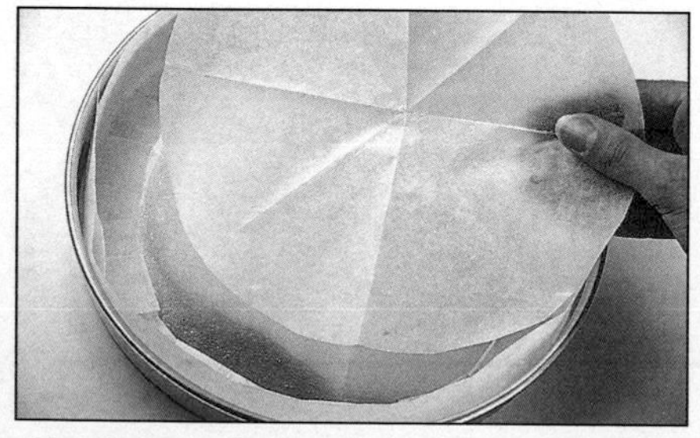

Line base and sides of a greased, round cake tin with baking paper.

Sift the flour, cocoa and spices over the nuts and fruit in bowl.

Stir the sugar and honey in a pan over low heat until sugar has dissolved.

Press the mixture out evenly in the tin, using wet fingers.

~ Hungarian Walnut Cake ~

Preparation time:
20 minutes
Total cooking time:
20–25 minutes

Makes one 20 cm round cake

3 eggs, separated
$1/2$ cup caster sugar
$1/2$ teaspoon vanilla essence
$2/3$ cup cornflour
1 teaspoon baking powder
$1/2$ cup finely ground walnuts

Coffee Cream
$1\,1/2$ cups cream
$1/4$ cup icing sugar
2 teaspoons instant coffee powder
2 tablespoons chocolate hazelnut spread
1 tablespoon coffee-flavoured liqueur

1~Preheat oven to moderate 180°C. Brush a deep 20 cm round cake tin with oil or melted butter. Line base with baking paper. Place egg whites in a small, clean, dry mixing bowl. Using electric beaters, beat until firm peaks form; add sugar gradually, beating constantly until sugar has dissolved and mixture has become thick and glossy.

2~Add egg yolks and vanilla; beat for a another 20 seconds. Transfer mixture to a large bowl. Using a metal spoon, fold in sifted cornflour and baking powder alternately with the walnuts; working quickly and lightly.

3~Spread mixture into prepared tin; bake for 20–25 minutes or until cake is lightly golden and shrinks away from sides of tin. Leave in tin 5 minutes before turning onto wire rack to cool.

4~**To make Coffee Cream:** Using electric beaters, beat combined filling ingredients until thick. Cut cake in half horizontally; spread one third of cream mixture over one layer of cake. Cover with second layer; spread remaining cream on top. Decorate with walnut halves and chocolate curls.

Variation~Slice one punnet of strawberries, reserving four berries for decoration. Beat $1\,1/2$ cups cream until thick, combine one-third with strawberries. Spread over cake base. Cover top and sides of cake with remaining cream. Decorate with strawberries.

Storage time~Unfilled cake can be frozen for up to one month.

Add sugar gradually to beaten egg whites, beating constantly until thick and glossy.

Fold in cornflour and baking powder alternately with the walnuts.

Bake the cake until it is lightly golden and shrinks away from the side of the tin.

Spread a third of the cream mixture over one layer of the cake.

~ Dundee Cake ~

Preparation time:
30 minutes
Total cooking time:
2–2 1/2 hours

Makes one 20 cm round cake

250 g butter
1 cup soft brown sugar
4 eggs, lightly beaten
1 cup chopped raisins
1 cup sultanas
1 cup currants
1/2 cup mixed peel
1/3 cup halved glacé cherries
3/4 cup slivered almonds
1 cup ground almonds
1 1/2 cups plain flour
1/2 cups self-raising flour
2 tablespoons brandy
125 g blanched almonds, for decoration

1~Preheat oven to slow 150°C. Brush a deep 20 cm round cake tin with oil or melted butter. Line base and sides with baking paper. Using electric beaters, beat the butter and sugar until light and creamy. Add the beaten eggs gradually, beating thoroughly after each addition.

2~Transfer mixture to large mixing bowl; add the fruits and almonds. Using a metal spoon, fold in the sifted flours and the brandy.

3~Spoon the mixture into prepared tin; smooth the surface. Arrange whole almonds on top of cake and press into surface gently.

4~Bake for 2–2 1/2 hours or until a skewer comes out clean when inserted into centre of cake. Leave cake in tin until completely cool.

Storage time~Cake will keep for up to two months. Wrap tightly in several layers of plastic wrap and store in the refrigerator.

~ Chocolate Mud Cake ~

Preparation time:
30 minutes
Total cooking time:
1 hour

Makes one 20 cm round cake

225 g butter
350 g dark cooking chocolate, chopped
1/3 cup warm water
5 eggs, separated
1 1/4 cups caster sugar
1 1/2 cups ground almonds
2/3 cup plain flour
1 tablespoon rum or brandy

Ganache
200 g dark chocolate, chopped
200 g butter

1~Preheat oven to moderate 180°C. Brush a deep 20 cm round tin with oil or melted butter; line base and sides with baking paper. Melt butter and chocolate in pan over low heat; add water, stir until smooth. Remove from heat, cool.

2~Beat yolks and sugar in large bowl until thick and pale. Using metal spoon, fold in chocolate mixture, then combined

Dundee Cake (top) and Chocolate Mud Cake

almonds and flour. Stir until smooth; add liquor. Beat egg whites in separate bowl until soft peaks form; fold into mixture. Spoon into prepared tin; smooth surface. Bake 1 hour or until skewer comes out clean when inserted into centre. Leave cake in tin 20 minutes then turn onto wire rack to cool.

3~To make Ganache: Melt chocolate and butter in pan over low heat; stir until smooth. Cool; stir occasionally until spreadable. Spread a third of Ganache on top and another third around sides of cake. Pipe rosettes or swirls around outer edges.

~ Coconut Cake ~

Preparation time:
20 minutes
Total cooking time:
40–45 minutes

Makes one 17 cm round cake

125 g unsalted butter
1 cup caster sugar
2 eggs, lightly beaten
1 teaspoon vanilla essence
$1^3/4$ cups plain flour
2 teaspoons baking powder
$^1/2$ cup milk

Orange Buttercream
$^1/2$ cup caster sugar
$^1/3$ cup water
125 g unsalted butter
2 teaspoons orange juice
1 teaspoon finely grated orange rind
$1^1/2$ cups shredded coconut or flaked toasted coconut to decorate

1~Preheat oven to moderate 180°C. Brush a deep 17 cm round cake tin with oil or melted butter. Line base with baking paper. Using electric beaters, beat butter and sugar in small mixing bowl until light and creamy; add eggs gradually, beating thoroughly after each addition; add essence; beat until combined. Transfer mixture to a large mixing bowl. Using a metal spoon, fold in the sifted flour and baking powder alternately with the milk; stir until combined and mixture is smooth. Spoon mixture into prepared tin, smooth surface. Bake for 40–45 minutes or until skewer comes out clean when inserted into centre of cake. Leave cake in tin for 10 minutes before turning onto wire rack to cool.

2~**To make Orange Buttercream:** Combine sugar and water in small pan, stir constantly over low heat until sugar is dissolved. Bring to boil, reduce heat, simmer without stirring, uncovered, 5 minutes. Remove from heat; cool. Using electric beaters, beat butter, juice and rind in small mixing bowl until light and creamy. Pour cooled syrup onto creamed mixture, beating until all has been added and mixture is smooth and fluffy. Spread top and sides of cake with mixture. Carefully press shredded coconut thickly around sides and top of cake, or decorate top with flaked coconut, if you prefer.

Storage time~This cake will keep for up to three days in an airtight container in the refrigerator or, without icing, for up to two months in the freezer.

Note~If you would like to layer the cake and spread Buttercream between the layers and on top of the cake, you will need one and a half times the quantities of ingredients listed for the Orange Buttercream. After Step 1, allow the cake to cool completely. Make Buttercream as described in Step 2. Cut the cake in half horizontally with a serrated knife and spread Buttercream on bottom layer. Replace top layer and spread with Buttercream.

Fold in the sifted flour and baking powder alternately with the milk.

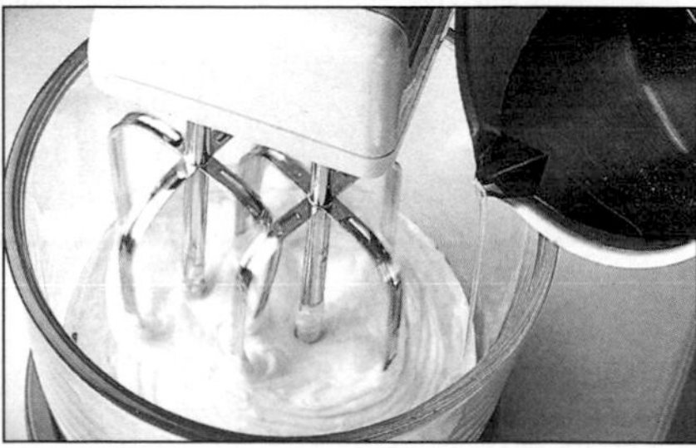

Pour cooled syrup onto the creamed mixture and beat until smooth and fluffy.

~ Apple Loaf Cake ~

Preparation time:
25 minutes
Total cooking time:
1 hour 15 minutes

Makes one loaf

125 g butter
2/3 cup soft brown sugar
1 egg, lightly beaten
1 teaspoon vanilla essence
1 medium green apple, grated
1 cup plain flour
1 cup self-raising flour
2 teaspoons ground cinnamon
1/4 cup milk
1 medium green apple, extra
1/4 cup apricot jam

1~Preheat oven to moderate 180°C. Brush a 21 x 14 x 7 cm loaf tin with oil or melted butter, line base and sides with baking paper. Using electric beaters, beat butter and sugar in a small bowl until they are light and creamy. Add the beaten egg gradually, beating thoroughly after each addition. Add essence and mix well.

2~Transfer mixture to a large bowl; add grated apple. Using a metal spoon, fold in sifted dry ingredients alternately with milk, stir until just combined and mixture is smooth. Spoon into prepared tin, smooth surface.

3~Peel, core and thinly slice extra apple. Arrange slices on top of cake mixture. Bake for 1 hour and 15 minutes or until a skewer comes out clean when inserted into centre of cake. Stand in cake tin 5 minutes then, using paper, lift out of tin and place on a wire rack to cool. Warm and sieve apricot jam, brush over top of cake.

Storage time~Will keep for two days in an airtight container. Not suitable for freezing.

~ Sultana Cake ~

Preparation time:
20 minutes
Total cooking time:
1 1/4–1 1/2 hours

Makes one 20 cm cake

250 g butter
1 cup caster sugar
3 eggs, lightly beaten
2 teaspoons grated lemon rind
1 teaspoon vanilla essence
2 cups sultanas
3 cups plain flour
1 1/2 teaspoons baking powder
2/3 cup buttermilk

1~Preheat oven to moderately slow 160°C. Line base and sides of a deep 20 cm square cake tin with baking paper.

2~Using electric beaters, beat butter and sugar in small mixing bowl until light and creamy; add eggs gradually, beating thoroughly after each addition; add rind and essence; beat until combined. Transfer

Apple Loaf Cake (top) and Sultana Cake

mixture to a large mixing bowl.

3~Using a metal spoon, fold in sultanas, sifted flour and baking powder alternately with milk; stir until combined and the mixture is smooth. Spoon mixture evenly into prepared tin; smooth surface. Bake cake for 1 1/4–1 1/2 hours or until skewer comes out clean when inserted into centre of cake. Leave cake in tin 20 minutes before turning onto wire rack. Serve cut into slices and spread with butter, if desired.

Storage time~Cake is best eaten within one week of making. Store in an airtight container.

~ Bienenstich (Beesting Cake) ~

Preparation time:
40 minutes +
1 hour standing
Total cooking time:
45 minutes

Makes one 20 cm round cake

7 g sachet dried yeast
40 g butter, softened
3/4 cup warm water
1/4 cup caster sugar
pinch salt
2 cups plain flour

Topping
60 g butter
1/2 cup caster sugar
1 tablespoon honey
1/2 cup flaked almonds

Custard
2 tablespoons custard powder
2 tablespoons sugar
1/2 cup milk
1/2 cup thick cream
1/2 cup sour cream
2 teaspoons vanilla essence

1~Brush a deep, 20 cm round cake tin with oil or melted butter. Line base and sides with baking paper. Combine yeast, butter, water, sugar, salt and 1 1/2 cups flour in large bowl. Stir until smooth and free of lumps. Cover with plastic wrap and leave in a warm place for 10–15 minutes. Add remaining flour, stir until almost combined. Turn onto lightly floured surface, knead 2–3 minutes or until smooth. Place in large, lightly oiled bowl; cover with plastic wrap. Leave to stand in a warm place for 20 minutes.

To make Topping: Combine butter, sugar and honey in small pan. Stir over low heat without boiling until butter has melted and sugar has dissolved. Bring to boil, reduce heat, simmer for 2–3 minutes. Remove from heat, stir in almonds; cool. Turn dough onto lightly floured surface, knead 2 minutes or until smooth. Roll out to form a 20 cm circle. Place in tin. Carefully spread topping over dough without stretching surface. Cover with plastic wrap, leave in warm place for 20–25 minutes, or until dough has risen almost to top of tin. Bake in preheated moderate 180°C oven for 35–45 minutes, or until a skewer comes out clean when inserted into centre and cake is golden brown. Leave in tin for 10 minutes before turning onto wire rack to cool. Turn top-side up.

To make Custard: Blend custard powder and sugar in medium pan. Gradually add milk, stir until smooth. Stir over medium heat until mixture boils and thickens. Remove from heat, transfer to medium bowl. Cover surface with plastic wrap to prevent skin forming. Cool completely.

2~To assemble the cake, cut it in half horizontally, place base on serving platter. Beat custard with electric beaters 1 minute. Add creams and essence; beat until smooth and creamy. Spread over cake. Top with other cake half. Cut into wedges to serve.

Note~Cake may sink slightly when three-quarters cooked. This is normal—the almond mixture can cause small, heavy pockets to form on surface. If this happens, gently scoop out excess mixture with teaspoon; continue cooking.

Carefully spread topping mixture over dough without stretching surface.

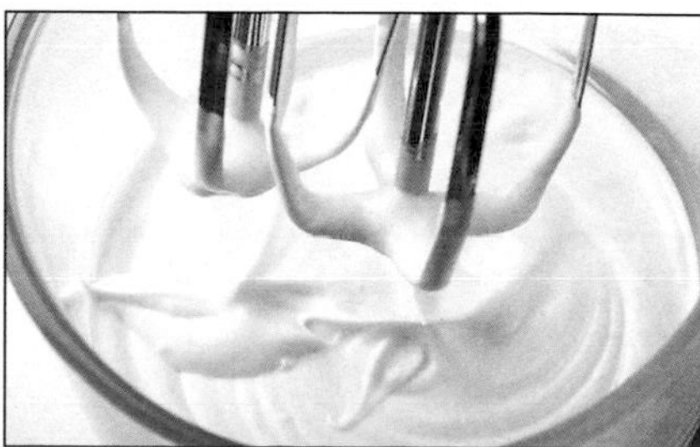

Add creams and essence to custard and beat until smooth and creamy.

~ Sacher Torte ~

Preparation time:
40 minutes
Total cooking time:
40 minutes

Makes one 20 cm round cake

125 g butter
1/2 cup caster sugar
4 eggs, separated
125 g dark chocolate, melted and cooled
2/3 cup plain flour
2 tablespoons apricot jam

Ganache
150 g dark chocolate, chopped
1/4 cup cream

1~Preheat oven to moderate 180°C. Brush a 20 cm round cake tin with oil or melted butter, line base and sides with baking paper. Using electric beaters, beat butter and sugar until light and creamy. Add egg yolks one at a time, beat thoroughly between each addition.

2~Add chocolate, beat until combined. Transfer mixture to medium bowl. Using a metal spoon, fold in sifted flour. Place egg whites in a small, clean, dry mixing bowl. Using electric beaters, beat until soft peaks form. Using a metal spoon, fold egg whites into chocolate mixture.

3~Spoon mixture into prepared tin, smooth surface. Bake for 40 minutes, or until a skewer comes out clean when inserted into centre of cake. Leave cake in tin for 15 minutes before turning out onto a wire rack to cool. Warm jam in a small pan, or microwave until it becomes liquid; strain through a small sieve. Place cake upside down on wire rack so that base is uppermost; brush evenly with jam.

4~**To make Ganache:** Combine chocolate and cream in small pan. Stir over low heat until chocolate has melted and mixture is smooth. Remove from heat, cool slightly. Pour ganache evenly over the cake, reserving about 2 tablespoons. Place reserved ganache into small paper piping bag and pipe the word "Sacher" onto the cake. Leave to set.

Storage time~This cake will keep for up to one week in an airtight container.

Hint~Ganache can be made with less chocolate and more cream and used as a light, delicious filling for cakes.

Add egg yolks one at a time to beaten butter and sugar mixture.

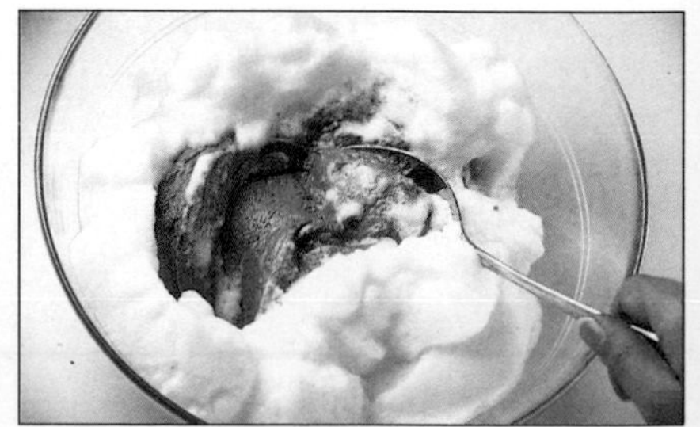

Fold the beaten egg whites into the chocolate mixture.

Brush surface of cooled cake evenly with warmed jam.

Pour ganache evenly over cake, keeping about 2 tablespoons for decoration.

~ Banana Cake ~

Preparation time:
20 minutes
Total cooking time:
1 hour 10 minutes

Makes one 20 cm round cake

125 g butter
1/2 cup caster sugar
2 eggs, lightly beaten
1 teaspoon vanilla essence
1 1/2 cups mashed ripe banana (about 4 medium)
1 teaspoon bicarbonate of soda
1/2 cup milk
2 cups self-raising flour

Butter Frosting
125 g butter
3/4 cup icing sugar
1 tablespoon lemon juice
1/4 cup flaked coconut, toasted

1~Preheat oven to moderate 180°C. Brush 20 cm round cake tin with oil or melted butter, line base with baking paper. Using electric beaters, beat butter and sugar in small mixing bowl until light and creamy. Add eggs gradually, beating thoroughly after each addition. Add essence and mashed banana, beat until combined.

2~Transfer mixture to a large mixing bowl. Dissolve soda in milk. Using a metal spoon, fold in sifted flour alternately with milk. Stir until all ingredients are just combined and the mixture is smooth. Spoon into prepared tin; smooth the surface. Bake for 1 hour or until a skewer comes out clean when inserted into centre of cake.

3~Leave cake in tin for 10 minutes before turning onto a wire rack.

4~**To make Frosting:** Using electric beaters, beat butter, icing sugar and lemon juice until smooth and creamy. Spread onto cooled cake, sprinkle with toasted coconut flakes.

Storage time~One week in an airtight container, or one month in freezer, un-iced.

Hint~Very ripe bananas are best for this recipe as they have the most developed flavour. Decorate with untoasted coconut, if you prefer.

Add vanilla essence and mashed banana to butter and sugar mixture.

Fold in the sifted flour alternately with the milk, using a metal spoon.

When cake is cooked, remove from oven and turn onto a wire rack to cool.

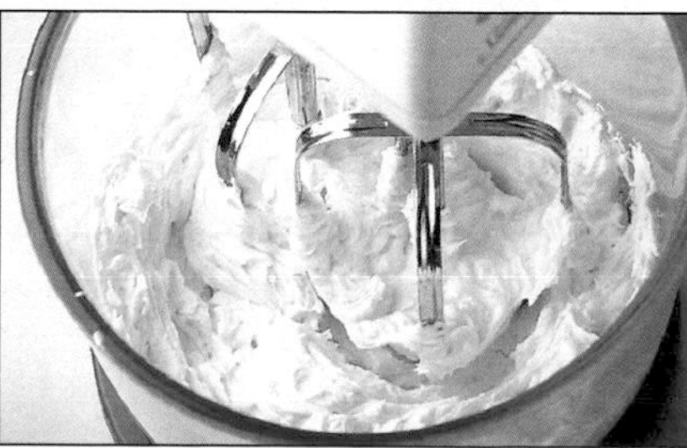

Beat butter, icing sugar and lemon juice until smooth and creamy.

~ Battenberg Cake ~

Preparation time:
40 minutes
Total cooking time:
20 minutes

Makes one 20 cm oblong cake

150 g butter
3/4 cup caster sugar
3 eggs, lightly beaten
1 teaspoon vanilla essence
1/2 cup ground almonds
1 3/4 cups self-raising flour
red food colouring
400 g commercial marzipan
1/2 cup apricot jam
2 tablespoons brandy

1~Preheat oven to moderate 180°C. Brush a shallow 30 x 25 x 2 cm Swiss roll tin with oil or melted butter. Line the base and sides with baking paper. Place a strip of foil down the centre of the tin, dividing it into two. Using electric beaters, beat butter and sugar in small mixing bowl until light and creamy; add eggs gradually, beating thoroughly after each addition; add essence; beat until combined. Transfer to large mixing bowl. Using metal spoon, fold in almonds and sifted flour; stir until ingredients are combined and mixture is smooth. Spread half the mixture into one divided half of tin; smooth the surface. Add a few drops of red colouring to other half of mixture, mix well. Spread pink mixture into other half of tin; smooth surface. Bake cake for 20 minutes or until skewer comes out clean when inserted in centre. Leave cake in tin for 10 minutes then turn onto wire rack to cool.

2~To assemble cake, cut white half into three equal slices, repeat with the pink half; trim ends. Between 2 sheets of baking paper, roll the marzipan out into a rectangle to fit the length of the cake and four times the width of one side. Place 1 strip of cake on top of the marzipan. Combine the apricot jam and brandy in a small pan and warm gently over low heat. Brush mixture onto cake strip. Place alternate coloured strip next to it, continue to apply jam and brandy, and layer the remaining strips to form a chequerboard pattern. Brush the long sides of the cake with jam and brandy. Wrap marzipan around the cake to cover all sides, leaving the ends open. Pinch the top edge of the marzipan to make a fluted pattern. With a sharp knife, score a diamond pattern on top of the cake.

Storage time~This cake is best eaten within one week of making. Keep it wrapped in foil in the refrigerator. Without the marzipan coating, the cake can be stored in the freezer for up to two months.

Note~This cake is of traditional German origin. The source of the name is obscure: some say the cake was first made for the wedding of Prince Henry of Battenberg, others that it was simply called after the Prussian village of the same name.

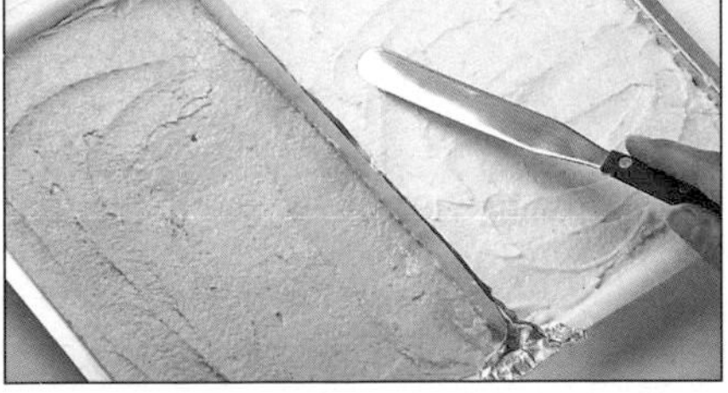

Smooth the surface of cake mixture on both sides of Swiss roll tin.

Brush long sides of cake with the warmed apricot jam and brandy mixture.

~ American Fruit Cake ~

(Stained Glass Window Cake)

Preparation time:
30 minutes
Total cooking time:
1½ hours

Makes one 20 cm ring cake

1 cup glacé cherries
½ cup chopped glacé apricots
¼ cup chopped glacé pineapple
¼ cup chopped glacé ginger
1 cup brazil nuts
1 cup walnuts
2 tablespoons Grand Marnier
½ cup plain flour
½ teaspoon baking powder
60 g butter, melted
1 egg
2 tablespoons soft brown sugar
¼ cup apricot jam
1 teaspoon Grand Marnier, extra

1~Brush a 20 cm ring tin with oil or melted butter; line base and sides with baking paper. Place glacé fruits and nuts in a large mixing bowl. Sprinkle Grand Marnier over fruit and nuts, combine. Leave to stand for 1 hour, stirring occasionally.

2~Add sifted flour and baking powder to mixing bowl. Whisk butter, egg and sugar together, add to fruit and nut mixture and stir until combined.

3~Spoon into prepared tin and smooth surface with a wetted hand. Bake in a preheated, moderately slow 160°C oven for 1½ hours or until cake is firm to the touch. Leave cake in tin for 30 minutes before turning onto a wire rack to cool.

4~Warm jam in small pan or in a microwave until liquid. Strain through a small sieve; stir in Grand Marnier. Brush over top and sides of cake while jam mixture is still warm.

Storage time~Cake will keep in an airtight container in the refrigerator for a period of up to three months.

Variation~Other fruits, such as glacé peaches, or nuts such as pecans or hazelnuts, may be used, if desired. Serve cake thinly sliced.

Note~This cake, wrapped and tied with ribbon, makes an attractive homemade Christmas gift for family or friends.

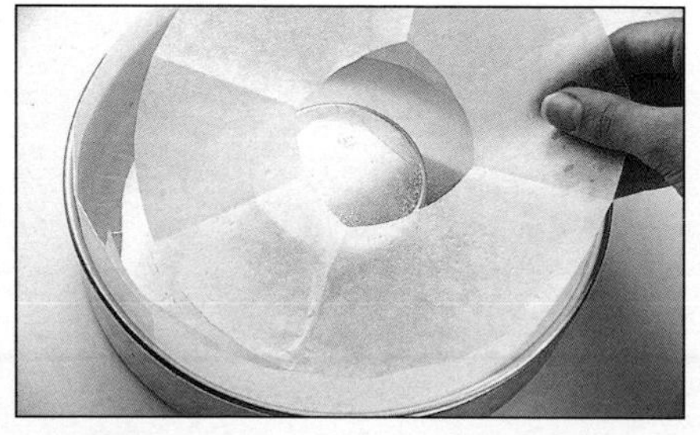

Line base and sides of greased ring tin with baking paper.

Add the sifted flour and baking powder to the fruit mixture.

Use wetted hand to smooth the surface of cake mixture in pan.

Brush top and sides of cake with jam and Grand Marnier mixture.

~ Celebration Fruit Cake ~

Preparation time:
1 hour
Total cooking time:
3 1/2 hours

Makes one 23 cm square cake

1 kg mixed dried fruit
3/4 cup chopped dried figs
1 cup chopped dates
1 cup chopped glacé cherries
1 cup mixed peel
2/3 cup rum
375 g butter
1 1/2 cups soft brown sugar
6 eggs, lightly beaten
1/2 cup apricot jam
2 cups plain flour
1 cup self-raising flour
3 teaspoons mixed spice

Fondant Icing
1 kg pure icing sugar
1 tablespoon gelatine
1/4 cup water
1/2 cup liquid glucose
1 tablespoon glycerine
1 cup pure icing sugar, extra

750 g marzipan
1/2 cup apricot jam, extra
2 egg whites, lightly beaten

1~Preheat oven to slow 150°C. Brush a 23 cm square cake tin with oil or melted butter, line base and sides with baking paper. Place all fruit in a large bowl, add rum, stir to combine thoroughly. Using electric beaters, beat butter and sugar in a small bowl until light and creamy. Add eggs gradually, beating thoroughly after each addition. Add jam; beat until combined. Add butter mixture to fruit, stir to combine. Using a metal spoon, fold in sifted flours and spice until just combined. Spoon mixture evenly into prepared tin; sprinkle top with cold water, smooth with wetted hand. Tap cake tin gently on bench top to settle mixture. Wrap a double thickness of brown paper around tin and secure with a paper clip. Bake for 3 1/2 hours or until skewer comes out clean when inserted in centre. Leave cake in tin until completely cold before turning out.

2~To make Fondant Icing: Sift icing sugar into large mixing bowl. In a small pan, combine gelatine with cold water. Add glucose, place over gentle heat until the gelatine has completely dissolved. Remove from heat, stir in glycerine. Cool 1 minute. Make a well in centre of icing sugar, pour in gelatine mixture. Use a wooden spoon, combine thoroughly. Knead by hand until mixture forms a firm, dough-like paste. Turn mixture onto a smooth surface lightly dusted with extra icing sugar. Knead well until smooth and pliable—mixture should resemble plasticine. Cover fondant securely with plastic wrap until required; do not refrigerate.

To cover the cake, place it upside down on large plate or covered board. Fill any small holes in surface with small pieces of marzipan. Warm and sieve jam; brush evenly over cake. Work the marzipan with hands until pliable, place on surface lightly dusted with icing sugar and roll out to 5 mm thickness. Lift onto cake with rolling pin, trim to fit cake and pinch corners to secure. Brush with egg whites.

Roll out fondant on a surface lightly dusted with icing sugar until about 7 mm thick—try to roll out to the shape of the cake. Lift onto the cake using rolling pin. Ease icing around sides and base of cake. Coat hands with icing sugar, rub top and sides of cake lightly until icing is very smooth. Cut away any excess icing from base with a small sharp knife. Decorate as desired.

Storage time This cake keeps well. Store for up to three months in refrigerator, wrapped in plastic wrap.

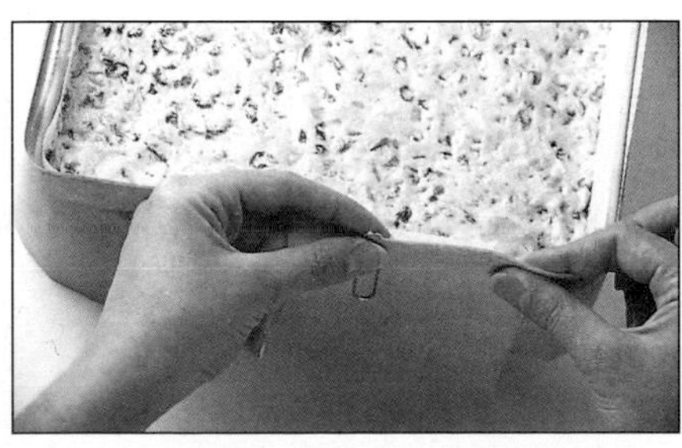

Wrap tin with brown paper and secure with a paper clip.

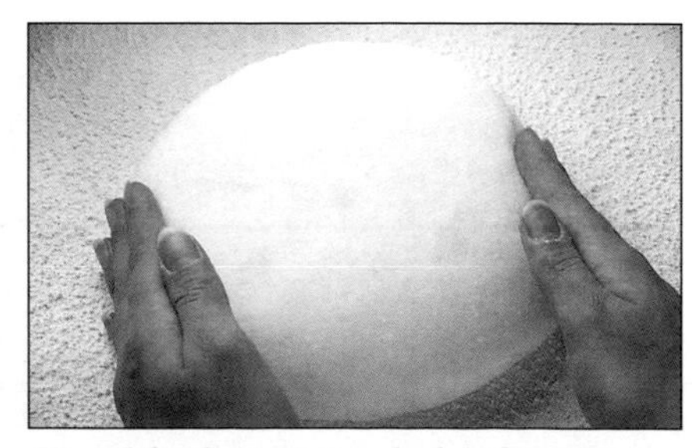

Knead fondant mixture by hand until it forms a smooth, dough-like paste.

~ Orange Poppy Seed Cake ~

Preparation time:
40 minutes
Total cooking time:
1 hour

Makes one 20 cm round cake

1/2 cup poppy seeds
2/3 cup orange juice
185 g butter
1/2 cup caster sugar
2 eggs, lightly beaten
3 teaspoons finely grated orange rind
1/2 cup self-raising flour
1 cup plain flour

Buttercream
2/3 cup caster sugar
1/3 cup orange juice
finely shredded rind from 1 orange
150 g butter

1~Preheat oven to moderate 180°C. Brush a 20 cm round cake tin with melted butter or oil, line base with baking paper. Combine poppy seeds and orange juice in small bowl. Using electric beaters, beat butter and sugar in a small bowl until light and creamy. Add eggs gradually, beating thoroughly after each addition. Add rind; beat until combined.

2~Transfer mixture to a large bowl. Using a metal spoon, fold in sifted flours alternately with the poppy seed mixture. Stir until just combined and mixture is almost smooth. Spoon into prepared tin; smooth surface. Bake for 45 minutes until a skewer comes out clean when inserted into centre. Leave in tin for 10 minutes, turn out onto a wire rack to cool.

3~**To make Buttercream:** Combine sugar and orange juice in a small pan. Stir over medium heat without boiling until sugar has completely dissolved. Add rind; bring to boil and simmer uncovered and without stirring for 5 minutes. Remove from heat, cool slightly. Remove rind from syrup with tongs, set aside. Cool syrup completely. Using electric beaters, beat butter in small bowl until light and creamy. Pour syrup slowly onto butter, beating until all is added and mixture is smooth and fluffy.

4~Cut cake in half horizontally. Spread one half with half the Buttercream. Replace top, spread with remaining Buttercream. Decorate with rind.

Combine the poppy seeds and orange juice in a small bowl.

Spoon mixture into prepared tin and smooth the surface.

Remove rind from sugar syrup with tongs and spread on wire rack to dry.

Cut cake in half horizontally and spread lower half with half the buttercream.

~ Pineapple Upside-down Cake ~

Preparation time:
20 minutes
Total cooking time:
40 minutes

Makes one 20 cm ring cake

20 g butter, melted
2 tablespoons soft brown sugar
440 g can pineapple slices in natural juice
90 g butter
1/2 cup caster sugar
2 eggs, lightly beaten
1 teaspoon vanilla essence
1 cup self-raising flour

1~Preheat oven to moderate 180°C. Brush 20 cm ring tin with oil or melted butter. Pour melted butter into base of tin, tip to coat evenly. Sprinkle brown sugar over butter. Drain pineapple, reserving 1/3 cup of juice. Cut the pineapple pieces into halves and arrange over brown sugar.
2~Using electric beaters, beat butter and sugar in a small bowl until light and creamy. Add eggs gradually, beating well after each addition. Add essence; beat until combined.
3~Transfer mixture to large bowl. Using metal spoon, fold in flour alternately with juice.
4~Spoon mixture evenly over pineapple; smooth surface. Bake for 35–40 minutes or until skewer comes out clean when inserted into centre. Leave in tin for 10 minutes before turning onto a wire rack to cool.

~ Jam Swiss Roll ~

Preparation time:
30 minutes
Total cooking time:
12 minutes

Makes one roll

1/2 cup self-raising flour
1/4 cup plain flour
3 eggs
1/2 cup caster sugar
2 tablespoons caster sugar, extra
1/2 cup strawberry jam
1/2 cup cream, whipped

1~Preheat oven to moderately hot 210°C. Brush a 30 x 25 x 2 cm Swiss roll tin with melted butter or oil, line base with baking paper, extending up two sides. Sift flours three times onto greaseproof paper. Using electric beaters, beat eggs in a large mixing bowl for 5 minutes, until thick, frothy and pale.
2~Add sugar gradually, beating constantly until completely dissolved and mixture is pale and glossy. Using a metal spoon, fold in flour quickly and lightly.
3~Spread mixture evenly into prepared tin; smooth surface. Bake for 12 minutes, until lightly golden and springy to the touch. Turn cake onto a dry, clean tea-towel covered with greaseproof paper that has been sprinkled with the extra caster sugar; set aside for

Pineapple Upside-down Cake (top) and Jam Swiss Roll

1 minute. Use the tea-towel as a guide and carefully roll cake up from short side, with the paper. Leave cake for 5 minutes or until cool.

4.~Unroll the cake and discard the paper. Spread with jam and cream and re-roll. Trim ends with a knife and serve sliced.

~ Simnel Cake ~

Preparation time:
40 minutes
Total cooking time:
$1^{3}/_{4}$–2 hours

Makes one 17 cm round cake

- **500 g commercial marzipan**
- **185 g butter**
- **1 cup soft brown sugar**
- **1 teaspoon grated lemon rind**
- **4 eggs, lightly beaten**
- **$1^{1}/_{4}$ cups self-raising flour**
- **$^{3}/_{4}$ cup wholemeal self-raising flour**
- **1 cup sultanas**
- **$^{1}/_{2}$ cup glacé cherries, halved**
- **$1^{1}/_{4}$ cup currants**
- **2 tablespoons apricot jam**

1~Preheat oven to moderately slow 160°C. Brush a deep 17 cm cake tin with oil or melted butter; line base and sides with baking paper. Roll out 300 g of the marzipan between 2 sheets of non-stick paper. Using a plate as a guide, cut out a 20 cm circle, cover and set aside. Repeat rolling and cutting process with remaining marzipan.

2~Using electric beaters, beat butter, sugar and rind in small mixing bowl until light and creamy. Add eggs gradually, beating thoroughly after each addition; add two tablespoons of the sifted flours to stop mixture curdling; beat until combined. Transfer mixture to a large mixing bowl; using a metal spoon, fold in combined flours including husks; add fruit; stir until combined and mixture is smooth. Spoon half the mixture into prepared tin; place the 200 g circle of marzipan over mixture, press down. Spoon remaining mixture over marzipan, smooth surface. Bake for 1 hour. Reduce oven to slow 150°C and bake for another 45–60 minutes or until a skewer comes out clean when inserted into centre of cake; remove from oven, cool.

4~Brush apricot jam over surface of cake. Place reserved circle of marzipan on top of cake; pinch edges to decorate; place cake under grill to lightly brown marzipan, then cool completely. Dust with icing sugar and decorate with coloured marzipan eggs, if desired. Tie a wide ribbon around the side of the cake.

Storage time~Because this cake does not contain alcohol and is iced with marzipan, it should be eaten within four weeks of baking. During humid weather, store in an airtight container in refrigerator.

Note~This English fruit cake is traditional Easter fare and was also served on Mothering Sunday, which fell during Lent. The top was sometimes decorated with twelve small balls, moulded from leftover marzipan, representing the twelve apostles. A small Easter chick often tops the marzipan eggs.

Top the marzipan circle with remaining cake mixture.

Brush apricot jam over the surface of the cooled cake.

~ Buttercake ~

Preparation time:
20 minutes
Total cooking time:
45 minutes

Makes one 20 cm round cake

125 g butter
3/4 cup caster sugar
2 eggs, lightly beaten
1 teaspoon vanilla essence
2 cups self-raising flour
1/2 cup milk

Buttercream
60 g unsalted butter
1/3 cup icing sugar
1 teaspoon vanilla essence

1~Preheat oven to moderate 180°C. Brush a 20 cm round cake tin with oil or melted butter, line base with baking paper. Using electric beaters, beat butter and sugar in a small mixing bowl until light and creamy. Add eggs gradually, beating well after each addition. Add essence; beat until combined.

2~Transfer mixture to a large bowl. Using a metal spoon, fold in sifted flour alternately with milk. Stir until just combined and mixture is almost smooth.

3~Spoon mixture into prepared tin; smooth surface. Bake cake for 45 minutes or until skewer comes out clean when inserted into the centre. Leave in tin for 10 minutes then turn onto wire rack to cool.

4~**To make Buttercream:** Using electric beaters, beat butter and sifted icing sugar together until mixture is light and creamy. Add essence, beat another 2 minutes or until mixture is quite smooth and fluffy. Spread icing over top of cake with a flat-bladed knife. Decorate with chopped almonds, or other nuts, if desired.

Storage time~ Buttercake will keep, iced, for two days in an airtight container in the refrigerator. It can be frozen, un-iced and wrapped tightly in plastic wrap, for up to one month.

Add eggs gradually to butter and sugar mixture, beating well after each addition.

After folding in flour and milk, stir until mixture is almost smooth.

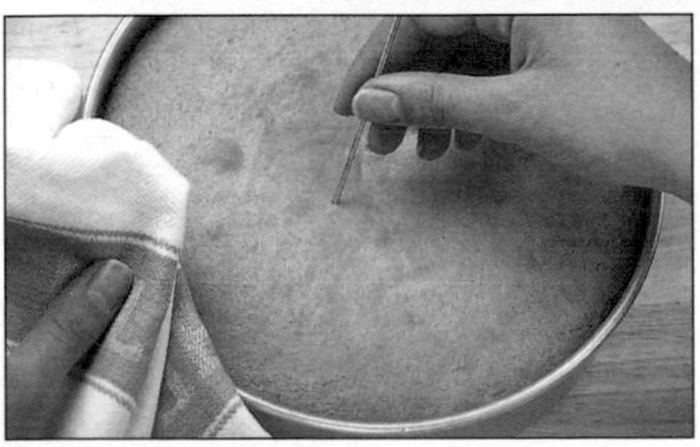

Bake cake until a skewer comes out clean when inserted into the centre.

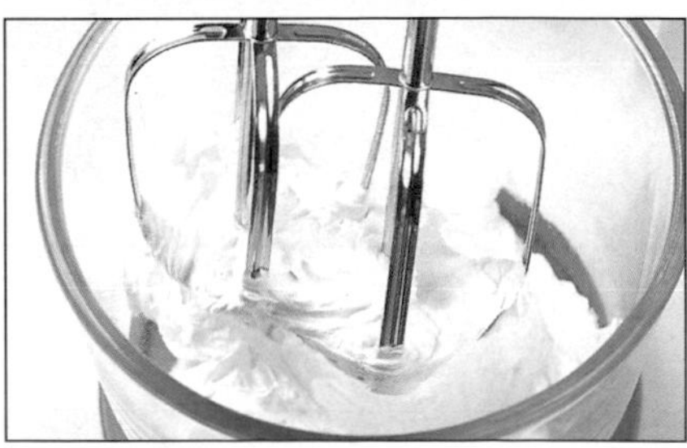

Beat the butter and icing sugar together using electric beaters.

Buttercake Variations

Cup Cakes

Prepare the Buttercake recipe up to the end of step 2. Line two 12-cup, deep patty tins with patty cases. Spoon level tablespoonsful of buttercake mixture into prepared patty cases. Bake for 10–15 minutes or until tops of cakes are golden. Leave cakes in the tin for 5 minutes before turning onto a wire rack to cool. Line the tins again with more patty cases. Repeat procedure with the remaining buttercake mixture. Makes 36.

Iced Cup Cakes

When cup cakes are cold, prepare Glacé Icing: Mix 3/4 cup sifted icing sugar, 2 teaspoons butter and 3 teaspoons boiling water to a firm paste in small heatproof bowl. Place over pan of simmering water, stir until smooth and glossy. Remove from heat, tint with food colouring. Spread a small amount of icing evenly over top of each cake. Decorate with coloured sprinkles or hundreds and thousands, or leave plain. Allow to set. Makes 36.

Butterfly Cakes

When cup cakes are cold, cut a small circle from the top of each one, cutting down to a depth of about 1–2 cm to allow for the filling. Cut each cake circle in half to make 'wings'. Spoon 1/2 teaspoon raspberry or apricot jam into each cup cake; top with 1 teaspoon whipped cream. Top with wings. Decorate with extra piped whipped cream, and jam. Dust with sifted icing sugar. Makes 36.

Marble Cake

Divide the buttercake mixture into 3 portions. Add 3–4 drops of red food colouring to one portion; stir until combined. Add 1 tablespoon cocoa powder and 2 teaspoons milk to the second portion; stir until combined. Place alternating spoonfuls of each mixture into a 20 cm round cake tin; swirl mixtures into each other with a skewer. Bake for 40–45 minutes or until a skewer comes out clean when inserted into the centre of the cake. Leave cake in tin 10 minutes before turning onto wire rack to cool. Ice as for buttercake, or with your favourite chocolate icing, if desired. Or dust top of the cake with combined sifted icing sugar and cocoa.

Marmalade Cake

Brush a 20 cm x 30 cm oblong tin with oil or melted butter; line base and sides with baking paper. Follow buttercake recipe to end of step 1. Add 1 extra egg and 1/3 cup marmalade to mixture. Continue to end of step 2. Spoon mixture into prepared tin; smooth surface. Bake in moderate 180°C oven for 25–30 minutes or until a skewer comes out clean when inserted into centre. Leave cake in tin 10 minutes before turning onto wire rack to cool. Make Glacé Icing as for Cup Cakes using lemon or orange juice instead of water. Add 2 teaspoons grated lemon or lime rind to mixture, stir until smooth. Spread evenly over top of cake. Decorate as desired and allow to set. Cut into squares or triangles.

From left to right: Iced Cup Cakes, Butterfly Cakes, Marble Cake and Marmalade Cake

~ Index ~